Real Talk Triple O One on One

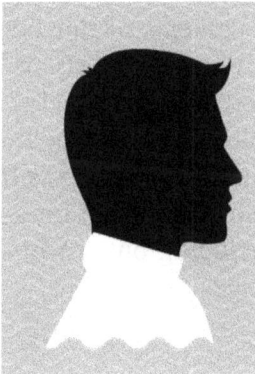

1 on 1

Can you handle it?

By
Drs. James & Angel Byrd

Purpose Publishing
1503 Main Street #168 ♪ Grandview, Missouri
www.purposepublishing.com

Printed in the United States of America

Book Editing by: Kershana Holiday & James Byrd
Book Formatting by Ella Carrol
Book Layout & Interior Design by Purpose Publishing
Book Cover Design by John Archer

Discounts available for bulk purchases of this book and set available by contacting us a www.flourishingarriages.com.

Dedication

We thank God, the Father, Son, and Holy Spirit for the wisdom, knowledge, and guidance in developing this counseling tool kit.

This book is dedicated to all marriages doing it God's way. God bless you as you take this journey together!

Table Of Contents

Introduction

Today, you are being introduced to something that could save the future of modern society as we know it. Perhaps you're thinking this is far too bold of a statement for any author to make, nonetheless, I'm willing to stand behind my claim. The fact of the matter is that our society as a whole is in dire straits, and the family unit is in steady decline like a row of falling dominoes. Something drastic must be done.

Having a happy home has become nothing more than an unattainable dream in the eyes of young people scarred by the destruction of divorce and fatherlessness. Something must be done not only for the sake of our families, but for the sake of future generations. If our grandchildren and their children after them are to have a fighting chance at maintaining thriving families, the solution starts with you today.

In a perfect world, every married couple would be assigned to Christian counselors that would aid in the renewal of their minds. In this same perfect world, each marriage would operate according to the principles of God and not the principles of man. Unfortunately, the world we live isn't perfect at all, in fact, it's quite the opposite. It would seem that if Christian counseling for every couple is not an option, then there is simply no favorable solution in sight. Fortunately, in seemingly hopeless situations God always has a ram in the thicket. I believe the contents of this kit may just be that ram. If we can't bring your marriage to counseling, we'll just bring our marriage counseling to you.

Welcome to a wonderful new revolution in marriage counseling!

The Triple O Real Talk tool kit was designed with your marriage in mind. There are no two people who get married and have no issues, and ultimately, no need for problem solving. Problems arise between the best of people with the best of intentions concerning one another. The reason no marriage is exempt from problems is because no two people think exactly the same, if they did, one of them wouldn't be needed.

Misunderstandings are bound to occur. Ultimately, it's the way we process and respond to misunderstandings, not the misunderstandings themselves that negatively or positively impact our marriages. These things in turn affect our children and grandchildren for generations. If the marriage and family are affected, then without question, our neighborhoods, schools, churches, work places and society at large will all be affected. That said, in order to change society we must start by changing our marriages.

With marriage playing such a vital role in the success or failure of an entire lineage, I can't explain why so many couples underestimate their need for third party assistance in their marriages from time to time. But, that's life. Perhaps it has something to do with male pride; husbands not wanting outsiders to know the intimate details of their private lives, or not wanting to seem as though they are incapable of handling their own family affairs. Well men, let me be the first to tell you that not only can you not handle your business, but no one before you or since you has been able to handle theirs without some assistance from time to time either. If anyone attempts to convince you that, without help, their marriage is rock solid and flourishing in both the husband and the wife's opinion; guess what? They are either the help you need, or the liars you need to avoid.

If we can't convince you to come to counseling, we have given you a way to engage in counseling on a one-on-one basis with your spouse. No confidentiality fears to avoid, because you and your spouse are the only ones that will know what you're discussing. No setting appointments based on your counselor's availability, because the schedule will be on your terms. No budgeting for the cost of hourly sessions... unless you decide to charge each other. All you'll need is the courage to face your issues head on, the belief that a change is needed, and the willingness to be the one that may have to do the changing.

Needing to be real without being too raw for radio, we would phrase this challenge in a way that our listeners came to know and love. We'd urge them to be willing to "put on their big boy pants and their big girl skirts" and address the roots of their marital problems. Are you and your spouse ready to be naked with one another?

If you can overcome the fear of opening up and become vulnerable to your spouse while they are becoming vulnerable to you; you are a prime candidate for success with the Triple O Real Talk counseling guide.

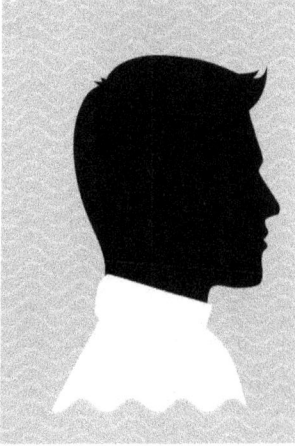

Frame of Mind Adjustment

Picture yourself in a battle for your marriage, but your opponent is not your spouse. Your opponent is every force that is against your union, and every characteristic about each of you that keeps you from working together.

With that said, you actually have two opponents opposing the success of your marriage union. According to Ephesians 6:12 *For we wrestle not against flesh and blood, but against principalities, against powers, against the rulers of the darkness of this world, against spiritual wickedness in high places;* our number one enemy is Satan himself along with all of the fallen spirits that fell from heaven with him. It is his number one goal to oppose whatever God is for. We know that God instituted marriage from the beginning way back in Genesis, so Satan is absolutely out to kill, steal, and destroy your marriage. Picture Satan, as enemy number one of your marriage and I will talk about enemy number two in a moment. Sometimes in marriage we only think Satan is in operation if there is extreme evil or darkness present and that is sometimes the case, but the bible says that Satan is cunning, crafty and even subtle. If someone wanted to destroy your marriage in the most crafty or cunning way it would not be with the loud and obvious signs that you would recognize. It has been said that the greatest trick that Satan ever played is allowing you to think that he doesn't even exist. This is how he dupes most marriages. There are things that go on in your marriage that keep you at odds all the time and often times they are subtle tricks of the enemy. Think about it; it's not normal for you to sometimes wake up in the morning and think thoughts like "I don't know why I married him/her; I think I married the wrong person; we might as well go ahead and get a divorce because we'll never love each other again or I wish he/she would just leave and never come back. Just think about it for a second; this is the man/woman you once thought that you couldn't live without and now you're having thoughts of ending it. It is in most cases a trick of the enemy to get you thinking like this because he knows that if you meditate on those types of thoughts long enough you will never be able to enjoy the kind of passion and love in your marriage that it possible.

As I said there is also another enemy opposing your marriage and the second major enemy to your marriage is your lack of knowledge. Don't immediately take that too negatively. I'm not saying that you are totally ignorant. You may be a medical doctor, a college professor, an engineer or a rocket scientist, but you may still lack the complicated knowledge of how to understand your spouse. Don't feel bad because most everyone lacks that knowledge. As a matter of fact this knowledge is not even present in some of the best marriages. You say "how can they have a great marriage if they lack the knowledge of understanding each other." That is a great question and sometimes the love of God and forgiveness factor will allow you to get over the speed bumps caused by the lack of knowledge in your marriage. Sometimes having enough fun times to compensate for the bad times will allow you to overcome. Every now and then you even have a couple that has an unusual chemistry together and they don't encounter too many speed bumps and with age sometimes couples just agree to not take the disagreements so seriously or so personal. Whatever the case may be, it is possible to have a measure of success without knowing how to really understand your mate, but for the majority of marriages, that is just not reality. Usually this lack of understanding how to deal with your spouse knowledgeably causes major withdrawals to the love tanks of your marriage. One of the ways to defeat this second enemy is by being able to communicate through the roughest times or in the deepest of conversations. You see anyone can talk about surface issues but it is when we have to hit the sensitive matters of our relationship that we end up either in a position of withdrawal & retreat or scratching and clawing at each other. Real Talk is here to help you rid that enemy; lack of knowledge, by obtaining knowledge of each other through intimate conversation. By obtaining knowledge of how to dwell at peace and harmony with each other you will also limit Satan's ability to attack your marriage union.

You must understand this time is set aside to let your guard down. Imagine yourself going under heavy sedation to prepare for major outpatient surgery. You will be cut; but it is only to remove what doesn't belong, or to insert what needs to be replaced.

Remember, you will heal from this session just as we heal from surgeries. It is okay for you to be nervous going in, but you are a very courageous person and you WILL NOT be ruled by fear.

I admit I had reservations my first trip down the road of Real Talk. Now, I am certain that it was one of the best experiences for my marriage; partly because of the results, and partly because it showed us that we could literally talk to one another about anything without hurting each other. We needed the freedom and increased intimacy in our marriage that comes with being able to communicate beyond the surface. I want to caution you. I know that most couples especially most men will go bonkers on the inside. I'm

14

going to call you out on the carpet right now men. I'll use myself as an example. When my wife first sat me down and said that she had some things she wanted to discuss, but she wanted to hear from me as the counselor and not me as the husband, my insides went haywire. I'm sure if I had been hooked up to any kind of machine that takes your pulse or heart rate, the machine would have actually exploded. I had no idea what she wanted to talk about, so the first thing that went through my head was, "What have I done and when did I do it?" You know they say that when you are faced with death, your life passes before your eyes. Well I can certainly say that in those few moments my marriage for the past week, month and year all passed before my eyes. I felt trapped because there was no one home but her and I. The television was turned off. We had no pressing agenda or place to go. She had me backed into a corner and usually when were backed into a corner we come out swinging, but this time was different. She calmly set the atmosphere and she told me that I could be honest and she would be honest, but we would make sure not to speak with malice in our hearts. If we had to use a knife to cut, we would make sure we numb the area real good first and then make the incision gently. We would cut away what needed to be removed and insert new pieces and stitch up the open wound right away. What started out as a scary proposition turned out to be the best hour, my marriage could have had at that time. It not only allowed us to deal with some things we needed to deal with but it showed us a new way to deal with things in the future. For some marriages this will be your lifeline. We know there are those marriages where it seems like you think and talk totally opposite about everything. That is just a trick of the enemy to get you focusing on your differences, to try and divide you. Believe me there are many things that you are alike at, because if there weren't you would never have fallen in love in the first place. Once your marriage is able to talk about difficult topics far beyond surface issues in a loving way, you will experience a closeness and intimacy not seen since the beginning days of your relationship. Believe me when I tell you, you will remember the day you had your first Triple O Real Talk One-On-One Session.

The next part of the frame of mind adjustment will be to make sure you have what it takes inside you to be able to forgive and love at the level needed to go deeper in your marriage. There is a level of forgiveness and love that you can only know if the one that gives it is residing on the inside of you. If you are not born again or saved as some would put it, you need to confess the prayer of salvation. Open your bible and read Romans 10:9-10 because if you confess with your mouth that Jesus is Lord and believe in your heart that God raised him from the dead, you will be saved. For with the heart one believes and thus has righteousness and with the mouth one confesses and thus has salvation.

Prayer of Salvation

If you do not know Jesus as your personal Lord and Savior, we invite you to pray the following prayer to receive Jesus into your heart.

God, Your Word declares in Romans 10:9 and 10, if I confess with my mouth Jesus is Lord and believe in my heart that You raised Him from the dead, I shall be saved. For it is with my heart I believe and am justified. It is with my mouth that I confess and am saved. Jesus, I receive you in my heart as my personal Lord and Savior.

The prayer you prayed is the first step. If you do not have a church home, we want to encourage you to get involved in a church that is preaching and teaching the uncompromising Word of God where you can be discipled and grow spiritually.

Pray Together

Now enter into prayer together. Before you get started, ask God to help you love your spouse as He (God) loves you, unconditionally. Pray that every word spoken will be spoken out of love.

Now is the time to pray specifically for your mate. Pray concerning things that will soften your heart towards them. For example:

God, thank you for blessing me with a spouse that has continued to love and endure with me. Set my spouse free from all fear so that he/she can share openly and receive true healing.   I pray that You would give me Your heart of compassion towards them, so that I'm careful not to become judgmental. Give me Your ears to hear the things they'll share with me, and Your wisdom to know if, when, and how to respond. God, I know that You are ultimately the only person that can give my husband/wife the healing he/she needs. Do what only You can do. Heal every hurt place, mend every broken piece, and restore every part of them that has been lost.

Feel free to pray concerning anything you feel led to concerning your spouse. This may even be a great time to go over the vows you made to each other on your wedding day. Just remember, this is not a "now *I lay me down to sleep*" type of prayer. This is serious business.

Chapter

2

Rules of Engagement

In our counseling practice we have ground rules that all couples must adhere to. The purpose of these rules is to establish safe boundaries. Without rules of engagement, in many cases, we'd find ourselves at war during these sessions instead of promoting peace in our marriages.

Today you can turn on the television almost any day of the week and see the wrong ways to handle tough conversations in marriage. There are now even reality shows getting ratings based on the wrong ways to handle marriage conflict. You see couples sitting before coaches or counselors, who allow, what are not the correct ways to communicate with each other and I'm sure most of you couldn't imagine being before a counselor screaming and cussing at your spouse. However, the fact that this is all in our faces can cause you to let your guards down and un-knowingly accept a little less than what you would normally. If you we're not as bad as what you saw on television, you could still be way out of bounds. Any hostility in your communication is not the best way to express love, compassion, forgiveness and to get understanding. You may have heard it said in times past that sometimes it's all right to blow off a little steam, but if that becomes a part of how you communicate with your spouse it will always be there and it will often come out at unwanted times. That is why you have to retrain yourselves with a new normal and rid yourself of the old ways. Rules of engagement are instituted for your protection and for the protection of your relationship. You wouldn't very well see one of the United States Military branches go off to war without any rules of engagement. Someone might just decide to pull the trigger at the wrong time and start World War three. Now I am not saying that you are going to war against your spouse. Quite the contrary; you are going to war with your spouse against the enemies of your marriage. We already talked about the main two enemies being Satan and a lack of knowledge, so this is a time for you to team up with your spouse and put together some rules that will allow you to go deep into the jungles of your marriage and come out a victor with absolutely no casualties of war.

It would be wise to take this opportunity to decide on a few rules of your own. Based on your knowledge of each other, add any rules you believe will help keep peace between you as you embark on this life changing journey. For example, some people find it helpful to lay back in a relaxed mode in order to stay calm.

While laying down is not a must, I certainly believe that there should be no standing or raising of voices. There should be absolutely no talking at the same time, or interrupting one another. Please allow your mate to finish complete thoughts before you prepare responses.

I believe I need to talk just a little bit about this point I just made. This is something you will have to train yourself to do. Everyone I know of including myself, starts preparing a response to something their spouse is saying, long before their spouse has completed the entire thought. What is dangerous about this is that you can't fully be listening when you are now preparing your own response. This is usually where listening turns into hearing only. Allow your spouse to finish complete thoughts and then before you respond ask them if there is more to what they are sharing. Ask them to dig deeper about why they are feeling the way that they feel. If you force yourself to dig deeper into your spouse's thoughts you will force yourself to become a better listener and not just a hearer only.

In addition, one of the most important things to remember is that your spouse's feelings are real or true to them, whether you agree or not. Even if you don't agree with what your spouse has to say, you cannot change the fact that their feelings are just as real to them as yours are to you. Our only hope for changing negative feelings is to find out the root of them and from there we can put a plan of action into place.

Failing to value your spouse's feelings is one of the biggest mistakes you can make in your attempts to communicate. When you fail to take your spouse's feelings seriously, it is as if you're telling them that you could care less about how they feel. If you've ever done this, you've made some serious deductions from the loving feelings you once shared. Do I believe that we should be ruled by our feelings in marriage? Absolutely not. Both your marriage and your love should be based on a decision, not a feeling. Feelings change far too often to allow them to be the determining factor in your decision to divorce or stay married. Making the decision to love your spouse the way God loves, without condition, will produce far more stability in your life and marriage. Nonetheless, the reality is that many of us are in fact ruled by our emotions, and since we are, this area needs to be addressed. While your marriage and your love should be based on a decision and not a feeling, once you've made your decision, good feelings will certainly make it easier to stick to the decision you've made. The more you lose that loving feeling toward your spouse, the harder it becomes to maintain the decision you made.

Sadly, most couples seem to have completely lost that loving feeling by the time they go down the road of marriage counseling. If this is you, I assure you that it's still not too late. Not only can you get those loving feelings back toward your spouse, but I will teach you how to maintain them forever.

Rules of Engagement
(Up front discussion)

- Share and note your *General Rules* with each other.
- Give a time frame for the discussion.

NOTE:
Your session does not have to take one hour,
but it's good to have an hour set aside.

No interruptions – cell phones, house phone, children, television, etc…Your sessions are not the time to multitask. The future of your marriage and family deserve your undivided attention. You are not washing clothes or cooking dinner during discussions. This requires and warrants focused concentration. Your remotes and smart devices should not be within arms reach. It may even be wise to shut them off completely so that the vibration of a silenced ringer doesn't distract your mind from the task at hand.

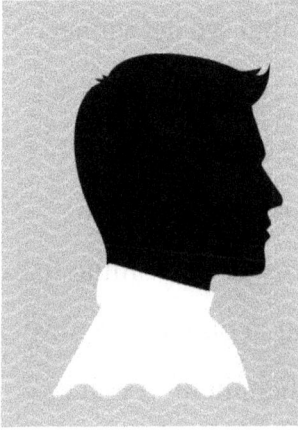

Chapter

3

Beyond the Surface

- For each of the next few chapters, list those items not visible to the natural eye that need to be discussed from your spouse's perspective.

- Use the "Path" section to number the items that need to be discussed. List them in order based on priority.

- Select your high priority items in each chapter.

- We have provided some examples for you to choose from if you are unable to come up with your own.

At this point it's going to be imperative that we get vulnerable before each other. In every marriage there are some taboo subjects. These are topics in your marriage that are marked fragile, handle with care. These are subjects that you may have tried to touch at times in the past but were very unsuccessful in coming to any kind of reasonable conclusion or agreement. You would know these subjects because when you've tried to touch them, it either ended up blowing up in your face or changing the mood from warmth to frigid. You know what I mean by mood swings. It's when everything can be going seemingly right and the wrong thing is said; all of a sudden it feels like this presence of heaviness comes over the room and you want to do the right thing but the wrong thing is now playing in your head. This is when the battle field of your mind is under attack. It's like the old cartoon's I used to watch when I was a kid. The little devil with a pitchfork would be on one shoulder whispering in your ear to take the wrong path, while the God like Angel would be on the other shoulder trying to get you to take the right path. This is usually when you deem a subject taboo, hands off, leave it alone or we'll try again some other time. Beyond the surface is where we bring those subjects back up, but now we discuss them in a healthy environment where the temperature can stay warm and the Angel of light gets the victory over the messenger from Satan. We will finally get victory over the tough subjects and finally get to unlock the key to that level of intimacy that we have never experienced before.

For right now you can list as many beyond the surface topics that you can think of and later in the "Path" chapter you can prioritize them in the order that you want to discuss them. Of course the most critical to either of you would be where you want to start. Don't think that you will get to, too many topics at once. Most likely you will only be able to handle one beyond the surface topic at a time and most likely you will need to revisit that same topic for follow up sessions.

Your Men's and Women's guides are set up for you to discuss several topics in great depth. Once you have compiled a list and prioritized them in the order of most importance, you will be able to use the guide books as your counseling notebook. The reason that there is a men's guide and a woman's guide is so that you can keep your notes and thoughts private, just as a professional counselor would. Remember you are attempting to act as your spouse's personal counselor. Your spouse should not be reading what you write in your guide.

When you get to the marriage tree with branches of listed issues that go on in many marriages, you can use that as a resource to help jog your memory about some of the past or present issues that you deal with in your marriage. The mind often has a way of trying to hide the painful situations that we have experienced. It's sort of a self-help tool in our minds, but we want to uncover them so that they are not just lying dormant, but they can be destroyed.

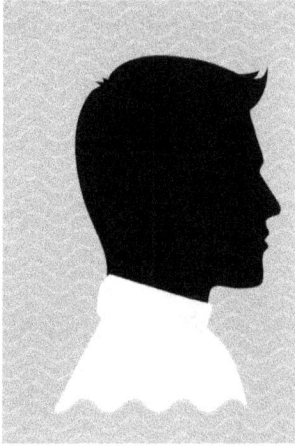

Chapter

4

His & Her Underlying Symptoms

What are some possible underlying symptoms that led to the concerns identified?

Now that you have identified some concerns or issues that you want to address in your marriage, we want you to go a little bit deeper. As your spouse's counselor, we don't want you to just look at addressing what they say the problem is, but we want you to dig deep until you can find the underlying symptoms that may actually be responsible for what they think the problem is. For example, a husband may feel that his wife is disrespectful at times to him as the man of the house, but the underlying symptoms may be her lack of respect for her father who treated her mother badly. She may have said in her heart as a young girl, "I'll never let a man dog me out like that." If the husband doesn't know about the relationship she had with her father or maybe a step-father, he may be fighting a losing battle that could easily be changed in time. The toughest part about an underlying symptom is not correcting it once you discover it, but actually discovering it is the tougher problem. The reason it is such a problem is because many times it was edged in us at a young and impressionable age, so we don't even remember or know that it happened. When we actually discover it, it's kind of like an ah ha moment. I can remember a time when I was driving to work one day and I heard a radio program in which the speaker was talking about getting over the pain of not having his father around to attend his sporting and school events as a child. I had never even thought about it, but I went back down memory lane as a young athlete in high school who played quarterback in football, point guard in basketball, sprinter in track and third baseman in baseball and I couldn't remember one occasion where my father was in the stands cheering me on. I don't know if he was ever there or not; maybe he was a time or two and I just don't recall it, but playing as much sports as I did and being very successful, there were an abundance of opportunities for him to be there and for me to remember; but I couldn't remember not a one. Now my parents divorced when I was thirteen and I lived with my mom, but we were in the same city as my father and I still couldn't remember one time. Immediately, such feelings of hurt and disappointment rose up inside of me that I began to cry right in my car. I happened to be in bible school at the time and I dealt with the pain and symptoms in my crisis counseling class. I wrote a letter of forgiveness to my father and I read it aloud in my class. It was even the first time that my wife had heard anything about it. Fortunately for me it didn't send me into a tailspin as a father myself of three children, but I can say that it probably had something to do with the fact that I like to be at everything my children participate in. I may at times even get too involved with their activities, but the point of the story is that neither I, nor my wife had any idea that all of that bitterness was lying dormant inside of me from my childhood years.

These are the type of discoveries you can find if you search deep enough for the underlying symptoms. My wife and I always say "Everybody has a reason for the way they act." Once you delve into Real Talk, Triple-O style, you will discover things about your spouse that you never knew. With the help of the Flourishing Marriages Tree on the next page, start to compile a list of some things you think may be plaguing the further success of your marriage.

(Please list below)

♥

♥

♥

♥

♥

(See diagram, next page)

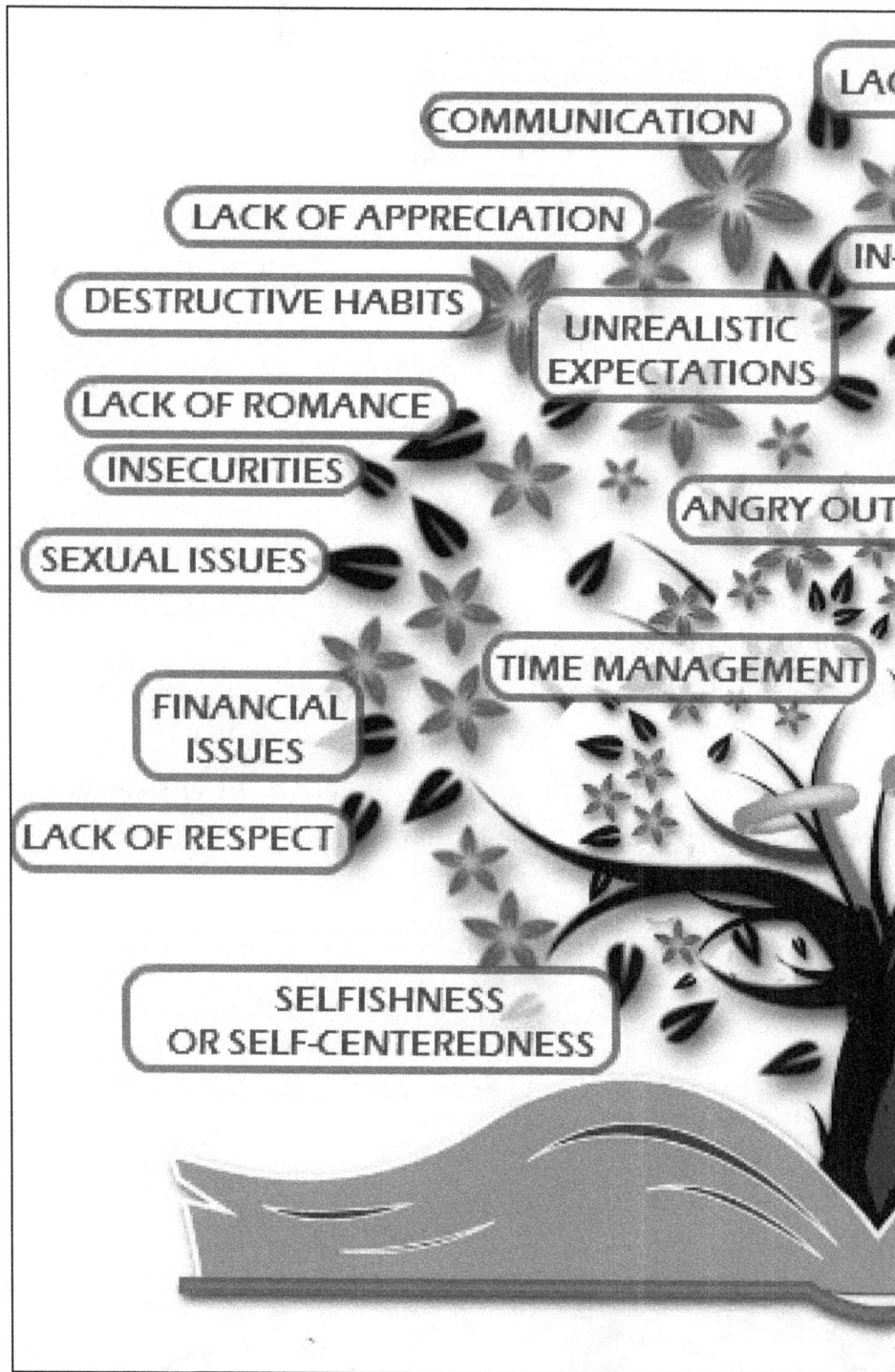

COMMUNICATION

LAC

LACK OF APPRECIATION

IN-

DESTRUCTIVE HABITS

UNREALISTIC
EXPECTATIONS

LACK OF ROMANCE

INSECURITIES

ANGRY OUT

SEXUAL ISSUES

TIME MANAGEMENT

FINANCIAL
ISSUES

LACK OF RESPECT

SELFISHNESS
OR SELF-CENTEREDNESS

CK OF ACTIVITIES TOGETHER

PRIORITY OF CHILDREN TO SPOUSE

-LAWS

LACK OF FAMILY COMMITTMENT

HOUSE WORK

UNFORGIVING

RELIGIOUS DIFFERENCES

BURST

NON-AFFECTIONATE

UNFORGIVING

GROWING APART

LACK OF HONESTY & TRUST

LACK OF UNITY

DISHONESTY

UNATTRACTIVE SPOUSE

FLOURISHING MARRIAGES LLC ®

I wanted to give just a little insight into some of the leaves on the tree. I'll start with a lack of activities together. Every couple needs to have things that they both enjoy doing together on a regular basis. People love having fun or doing what they like to do. If your spouse is not doing what they enjoy with you, they will be doing it with someone else. We encourage couples to eliminate most of the solo activities and replace them with activities the both of you enjoy. You may have to reach deep into the activity bucket to find things that you both enjoy, but your marriage and family is worth it.

The priority of importance between the children and each other is a major issue in many marriages. I often advise young couples to make sure they work on having a rock solid marriage before having children because children can steal your heart from your spouse. Children who steal the heart of a marriage for a long enough period of time eventually become first place and it's usually the husband that ends up looking for companionship elsewhere. Don't let the crumb snatchers, no matter how much of a blessing they are, steal your heart from your spouse.

In-laws can sometimes appear to be out-laws. You have to remember to leave and cleave. Your parents used to hold that number one spot in your heart but now that spot belongs to your spouse and you have to protect that number one spot with everything within you. The in-laws can't have it, the children can't have it, the friends can't have it and the job can't even have it.

Religious differences are a no-no in your marriage. When it's just the two of you it seems like it may not cause much of an issue, but when the children come a long you will fight over how you want to raise the children. I have seen many a relationship doomed over one parent wanting to raise the child as a Christian and the other not agreeing with that. I know this is a subject that needs to be covered before you say I do, but just in case you find yourselves in this situation, you must get agreement in the spiritual arena.

Lack of appreciation is something that can effect both of you but it really can do damage to a man. Men are notorious for gravitating to where they are the most appreciated. Many times it's with the job that he does well or a particular activity or hobby that he excels in. Men live for appreciation. The funny thing about it is that most of them don't even know it. It is something that just happens naturally and as naturally as they gravitate to appreciation, they gravitate away from a lack of appreciation. I'm not meaning to slight women in the area of appreciation. Women enjoy and need appreciation as well, it's just not as crucial to their psyche as it is to the man.

Unrealistic expectations in a marriage can lead to disappointment. If you expect things of your spouse that will most likely never happen, or if you expect things to happen to quickly, you are setting yourself up to be disappointed. In some cases it's almost better to have no expectations at all, so at least that way you won't be disappointed and if your spouse does something, you'll just appreciate it.

An unattractive spouse is going to fall more on the side of women needing to keep up their appearance than men. Just as before when I talked about men needing to be appreciated more, this time women need to be more attractive. It's kind of because men are more visual than woman. I am again not excusing the men from needing to keep up their appearance, but women are more relational where men are more visual.

Lack of romance is going to lean more towards affecting the wife. With women being more relational than men, romance is something that women absolutely need more than men.
Most men are only romantic during the chase and then it seems as if the romance gene is lost. You've heard it said "Whatever you did to get her, you'll need to do to keep her," and I agree with every word of it. I do, as a man, understand that this is normal for men, but men are also very habitual so if you work at it or train yourself to be more romantic for your wife's sake, you can.

Financial issues are major hot button issues in most marriages. The most important factor when it comes to finances is to make sure you are both on the same page. You must work together and agree in this area. Finances or the lack there of, can and does destroy most marriages; however spending all of your time chasing after money can also destroy your marriage. You have to have balance with your time as it relates to your marriage, family and careers.

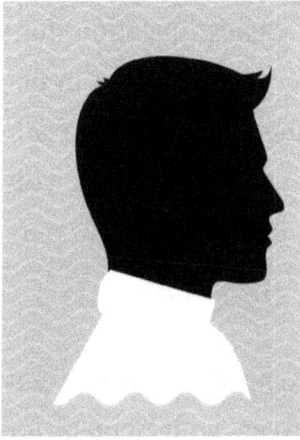

Chapter

5

Let's Set the Stage

The following questions in the "Let's Set the Stage" section will need to be addressed in each chapter of your men's & women's guides.

	Yes	No
Do you believe Jesus has forgiven me?	☐	☐
Have you forgiven me?	☐	☐
Are you willing to forgive yourself?	☐	☐

If no, address how you plan to move forward.

_____

_____

_____

_____

_____

_____

_____

Hopefully the first question will be the easiest question during each chapter. This question must be answered with a yes in order for you to even believe that there is a chance at forgiving each other. You must know that Jesus has forgiven you for anything you will ever ask him to forgive you for. He hung, bled and died to purchase that forgiveness.

The next question that you must deal with after every Real Talk session is whether or not you have forgiven your spouse for any injustices they may have committed, whether intentional or unintentional. As we talked about in the forgiveness section of the video, all of us at some time or another will and have needed to ask God to forgive us and the bible is clear that we can't even think that we can get God's forgiveness when we won't forgive our on brothers, sisters, mothers, fathers etc... We have to model Jesus when it comes to forgiveness because neither us, nor our spouses are perfect, so we will indeed need to be forgiven at some point in our future.

Finally, the question that comes next is about you being willing to forgive yourself. Now the bible doesn't speak about forgiving ourselves, but the real point that we are trying to make here is, if God has forgiven you and your spouse has forgiven you, don't live as if you're condemned. Some people hold on to the offenses they have committed against their spouse long after their spouse has let it go. If your spouse has let it go and God has let it go, there is no need for you to keep dwelling on it. It can only keep you from moving forward like you really need to.

These are essential steps in regaining the love you feel that you've lost. Forgiveness is a major piece. As believers, we believe in the "Jesus forgiveness" principle, which is to forgive your mate as much as they need you to. Still, we seem to find forgiving our spouses far easier than forgiving ourselves. You must be willing to forgive yourself in order to move forward and to treat your spouse the way they need to be treated.

Chapter
6

The Path

The "Path" consists of the topics selected, in order based on priority (referenced earlier on page 11). For each topic within each chapter, you will have an opportunity to discuss up to five bullet points. The following additional items should be noted as well: the response given by your spouse, the follow-up question, the solution agreed upon, and the action plan for improvement.

The five bullet points that you will cover with each topic you discuss is where the real counseling will take place. You will need to write what you hear your spouse saying. You don't have to write it word for word, but you want to write enough or write it in a way that when you look back on it at a later date you will be able to fully remember what they were trying to say. This plays a dual role, because it also kind of forces you to listen to what they are saying without preparing responses to what they are saying. The whole point of you acting as a counselor is so that you won't put up your dukes and be on the defense. Our natural defense mechanisms appear when we think our spouse is attacking our character, but since you are not acting in the normal role of the spouse but in the role of the counselor you can avoid the normal defense mechanisms.

With every topic discussed you should also be asking follow up questions. Usually more than one! Please pay close attention to what follow up questions are getting you deeper responses, because that may be the direction you want to go in most of the time when it comes to dealing with this sensitive material in your marriage. The fact that we are asking you to ask follow up questions means that you will use phrases like; how did that make you feel, when did you first start feeling like this, who was the person that caused these feelings you feel, what would you say is the thing you need to move forward in this area, and why do you think you normally react like this. Of course you can come up with your own, but this list is just to show you the how, what, when, why and where style.

The next bullet point that you want to address is the solution that the two of you agree upon. This is necessary for every subject you discuss. Marriage is supposed to be a union of two acting as one. Yes a man and a woman are coming together to form a single unit. Agreement is absolutely needed in every area of your marriage. A house divided against itself cannot stand. Wherever there is disunity, the enemy has a chance to get in a wreak havoc. If you have trouble getting agreement on any single issue, it is best not to make a final decision in that area, unless it is necessary for the safety of your family. As the head of my household, I try to discuss all issues with my wife and come to agreement on everything we deal with. If I have to make a decision that she doesn't agree with, it would never be a selfish decision, but one made out of love and concern for the wellbeing of my family. I want to drive this point home; when I say agreement in every area that means finances, child rearing, spiritual lives, eating habits, spending habits etc… Whatever you can think of, you can find agreement on it. Think of your marriage like a corporation and your issues like problems before the company in a board room. Get out the dry erase markers and keep coming up with possible solutions until you come up with something the two of you can happily agree on.

The reason you need to both happily agree is because the moment one of you fakes this agreement and something doesn't' go right, you'll have a tendency to say "I told you so, or I was never really in agreement with that in the first place." Agreement helps avoid finger pointing. If you have great success you both enjoy it and if you run into an occasional failure, you don't get at odds with each other, but you work together to dig yourselves back out of it. That's being unionized. That's marriage. That's submitting one to another. The wife submitting to her husband and the husband submitting to God and loving his wife like Christ loves the church.

Finally write out with clarity the action plan that you put into place for improvement. You can't just discuss your problems, but you have to come up with tangible plans for improvement. It usually takes three to four weeks to create new habits. Believe me when I say old habits don't die easily. Your current behavioral patterns are cemented into you and you will need to take a jack hammer and break up that cement and lay an all new foundation. If you can achieve these five steps with every issue that arises in your marriage you will keep Satan out and you will keep the lack of knowledge out of your marriage.

If there are additional topics that need to be discussed, feel free to purchase an additional journal for both you and your spouse (see product list on page 67).

Hers

♥

♥

♥

♥

♥

His

♥

♥

♥

♥

♥

Chapter

7

The Counselor

Now is when you officially become your spouse's counselor. You may be thinking, "I don't have a counseling background or any counseling experience", and while this is true, this section will equip you with the necessary techniques to effectively draw from what is inside your counselee. This may require several hypothetical scenarios and some role playing. While this type of practice may seem extreme, it's important to remember that although you are married, under these circumstances, your role is not the marriage partner but the role of a counselor. As the counselor, you will not ask questions or provide responses the way you would as a concerned spouse engaged in open dialogue with their husband or wife.

In your role as your spouse's counselor, you will serve them best by asking questions that usually are of the who, what, where, when, why and how variety. You see, the job of the counselor is not to tell the counselee what they need to do and how they need to feel; the job of the counselor is to simply discover what the counselee is feeling, why they are feeling it, when they started feeling it, who contributed to them feeling that way, and how do they plan to transform the feelings they don't want into feelings they do want.

As the counselor, you'll find that most issues are both discovered and resolved simply by allowing the counselee to talk through the origins of their feelings. Most answers or solutions are not given by the counselor, but they are discovered by the counselee themselves. Be aware that as both the spouse and the counselor you will have a tendency to want to slant your responses and questions towards your personal feelings. We strongly caution you away from operating with this type of bias. You will never get all of what you want out of a counseling session without honesty and non-bias motives. ***Remember, the most important thing is not to interject your feelings. The goal is a healed spouse. A healed spouse becomes a healthy spouse, and healthy spouses yield flourishing marriages.*** In this environment you may discover that you are the cause of some of your spouse's issues, and that's okay. It's far better to know this and have an opportunity to make adjustments, than to blindly lose a spouse to divorce.

One of the keys to being successful at this point is going to be understanding that this is absolutely not a competition between you and your spouse. It is not your object to win or lose.

This is more about how you play the game. I often say that three things can usually happen when you engage in real talk with your spouse; #1 you win the conversation, #2 they win the conversation, #3 you both win the conversation. Although I listed three things, there are really only two things happening. Either you both win or you both lose. Let me break it down a little more for you. If you win the conversation and your spouse loses; you both lose. If they win the conversation and you lose; you both lose. The only way for anyone to win is if you both win and the only way for you both to win is to end up in total agreement. This is why you can't be biased; you can't get wrapped up in your feelings. You have to be totally unbiased and working as a counselor for your spouse. If they sense any bias or any resistance to what they are revealing they will lock it up and you won't be able to get the key. I know that I am drilling some of this information into you, but how many times have you heard of some really good advice to use in your relationship to avoid major blow ups. I've heard people say take a time out; use key phrases that re-mind you to back off; table the discussion for another time; and even walk away and hope that it goes away. Nothing works when your spouse pushes your button. Before you know it, you've said some things that you wish you could take back. You've said some things that the voice inside of you was telling you not to say. You've flat out said some things that were down right ungodly. Bottom line is, when you are surprised and unprepared and your buttons are pushed, you are likely to react in the wrong way. That's why with Triple-O

Real Talk, we prepare the stage in advance. We change the roles that you are used to playing. We give you every opportunity to finally have success in the most sensitive of subjects.

The next thing I want you to do is take off your Mr. or Mrs. fix-it hat. Everybody always feels they have the answer to their spouse's problems. Normally you may, but I can't tell you how man times during our counseling sessions with other married couples, I thought early on I knew what the problem was and what the fix was only to continue talking and listening and discover more that I wouldn't have discovered had I jumped in with what I initially thought was the answer. I can't say it enough, you have to dig deeper. When you have finally dug deeper, then and only then should you dig deeper still. Finally again resist the temptation to know the answers. It is very possible that during these sessions you will discover things about your spouse that you didn't know even after being married for twenty or thirty years. The more you find out about your spouse and about why they are who they are and why that act the way they act, the more compassion will flow from you to them. It's an amazing process and it brings couples closer together. You can literally go from the brink of walking away from it all, to closer than you thought you'd ever be.

Journaling

On the lines provided in the journal you should avoid attempting to write down your spouse's responses word for word.

Instead, jot down highlights that will allow you to remember what was discussed. These notes will allow you to quickly review what was discussed, if and when follow up sessions occur, so that you have a base of knowledge to start from instead of asking all of the same questions.

The journals will also afford you the opportunity to read back through the information from time to time so that you can stay freshly in tune with your spouse and with what they have been dealing with. As you are listening to your spouse try not to look down at your journal the entire time. You want to stay engaged with them as they are talking to you, but you want to listen for key words or phrases that they might say and jot them down. You can always go back after the session is over and write complete sentences or thoughts. You definitely want to make sure that you go back the same day if possible because you want what they said to be fresh in your memory. If not, I promise you that you will lose details. I know at the time you are listening, you may think you'll remember everything, but you won't. It's best to go back over your notes as soon as the session has officially ended and finish all of your journaling.

Forgiveness

Before you develop your action plan for improvement, be sure to cover the forgiveness questions and be real with each other in your responses. Forgiveness is a major part of any marriage, and without it you can't move past issues successfully. Forgiveness doesn't necessarily mean you will forget the offense, but it does mean you will give up the right to sentence your spouse for the offense.

You choose not to be the judge and jury, and commit to never bringing up the offense again. The only instance where bringing up a past offense becomes appropriate under these circumstance is to bring help to someone else's union, or to serve as a testament to what the two of you have grown past.

In relationships, we have this ability to play judge when we feel that our spouse has committed an offense against us. We unknowingly put on an invisible black robe, we slam down an invisible gavel and we look to the jury of twelve peers, which happens to be the person we see in the mirror. We give them their sentence without necessarily saying one word. The sentence may be the silent treatment. We call the silent treatment, silent abuse. The sentence may be closing the wallet or closing your legs. We call that sentence witchcraft. The sentence may even be leaving and going to hang out with your friends. We call that sentence running from your problems. You never want to get into the habit of running because then when tough times come you will be used to running away and whatever you're used to doing in a tough time will come easiest. Forgiveness is giving up the black robe and the gavel. Forgiveness is saying, even though they are guilty, I pronounce them not guilty. Also, try and make a pact with your spouse that you won't bring up past offenses, once you've forgiven each other, of them. The only time my wife and I can bring up old offenses, is when it is to show another couple that we have overcome something similar to what they are going through, and even then, you should make sure it is o.k. with them.

Always remember to apply the Jesus principle of forgiveness in your marriage. This means forgiving your spouse as many times as they need to be forgiven. Only after forgiveness has taken place are you ready to formulate a true action plan for improvement.

Building an Action Plan

Once you have completed a session, it's best for the same spouse to remain the counselor until you've successfully worked through creating an action plan for one topic on the counselee's list before switching roles.

If you are starting in the role of the counselor and you are under the impression that you are going to switch roles during the same session that frame of mind would cause you to unknowingly speed things up, and that is not what you want because you are not in a hurry during these sessions. It is my opinion that you should go into one session expecting to deal with one issue for one person.

When finishing out a session, always remember to end on a high note by offering viable solutions you both agree upon, then pray together to seal the deal. Prayer is a powerful tool that bonds the two of you away from individualism into oneness.

It is our sincere desire that through these sessions you'll learn to fight for your spouse instead of against them.

Husbands and wives should be fighting for their marriages instead of for their rights. You should be fighting the things that war against your union, which are Satan and the culture he has created to cause couples to be divided. If you'll focus your fighting toward the right opponent, and fight the good fight of faith, in the end you will be victorious. Remember, God is the creator of marriage, and in order to understand how something works, you must always seek its creator. When it comes to marriage, God's way is flawless and man's ways are flawed.

God bless you; and here's to marriage happily ever after. ***Now get to work!***

As you delve into conversation with your spouse and take on a Counselor's role, your journal will serve as detailed study of your spouse. By the time you've filled its pages, you'll hold the only copy of an invaluable resource in understanding and adapting to your spouse.

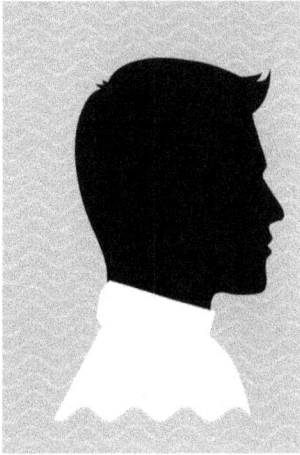

Chapter

8

DVD Time~ Her & His Declarations

Now it's time to go to the DVD. Please watch the DVD before signing your "Declaration", and before starting the work in your "Guide."

Her Declaration

I, _____, promise to listen to,

hear out, honor, and respect _____,

my bride, whom I came into covenant with on

_____, before God, our family, and

friends, as we delve into issues beyond the surface.

Sign

_____

Date

_____

His Declaration

I, _____, promise to listen to,

hear out, honor, and respect _____,

my bride, whom I came into covenant with on

_____, before God, our family, and

friends, as we delve into issues beyond the surface.

Sign

_____

Date

_____

Chapter
9

Scripture Prayers for Marriage

Scripture Prayers for Your Marriage

The following are short scripture prayers that you can use to pray for your marriage. These prayers are based on the Word of God. You can plead them with confidence and with faith.

Scripture Prayers

Father, I plead that we would speak the truth in love to each other, honestly and openly sharing our feelings with each other (Ephesians 4:15,25).

Lord, I pray that our marriage will glorify You and be an example of Your intention for marriage (1 Corinthians 10:31).

God, I plead that You would give us wisdom and compassion in dealing with our in-laws (Matthew 5:7).

Father, bless and strengthen our marriage in the midst of the pressure and problems of our lives (2 Corinthians 12:9).

Father, I ask You to protect our marriage from the attacks of Satan. Deliver us from his evil, destructive plans (1 Peter 5:8).

Father, grant that we might find great delight and joy in each other (Proverbs 5:18).

Lord God, I pray that You would deepen and strengthen our friendship to each other (Proverbs 17:17).

Scripture Prayers

Father, I plead that Your power would sustain and give stability to this marriage (Jeremiah 32:17).

Father, help us to discern and deal with those things that hinder and hurt our relationship (Psalm 139:23-24).

Father, I ask that our strengths would match and overcome our weaknesses (Genesis 2:20-23).

I pray that we would be kind and tenderhearted to one another, forgiving one another even as God Christ's sake has forgiven us (Ephesians 4:32).

I plead that we would be sensitive to the needs and hurts of each other. Enable us to minster to each other in these areas. (Matthew 20:28).

God, create within us a hunger for each other. Let us be satisfied with one another (Proverbs 5:19-20).

I plead that You would give us a heart to seek after You and serve You all the days of our lives (Psalm 63:1).

Scripture Prayers

Father, I pray that You would grant us the wisdom and power to gain and use our finances wisely (Proverbs 3:9-10).

Lord, I ask that You would deliver us from pettiness and forgiveness in our relationship (Matthew 18:20-21).

Father, I plead that we will surrender all that we are and all that we have to each other (Genesis 2:24-25).

I pray that we would love You with all our being and our neighbors as ourselves (Matthew 22:37-40)

Lord God, I ask that we would love and obey Your Word, building our lives, marriage, and family on its truth (Psalm 119:97).

Father, I plead that we would be patient with each other in all the circumstances of life (1 Corinthians 13:4).

1 Corinthians 13: 4-8 (New International Version) 4 Love is patient, love is kind. It does not envy, it does not boast, it is not proud. 5 It does not dishonor others, it is not self-seeking, it is not easily angered, it keeps no record of wrongs. 6 Love does not delight in evil but rejoices with the truth. 7 It always protects, always trusts, always hopes, always perseveres. 8 Love never fails.

1 Corinthians 13:13 (New International Version) 13 And now these three remain: faith, hope and love. But the greatest of these is love.

Scriptures for Marriage.

Marriage should be honored by all, and the marriage bed kept pure, for God will judge the adulterer and all the sexually immoral. (Hebrew 13:4)

The LORD God said, "It is not good for the man to be alone. I will make a helper suitable for him." (Genesis 2:18, NIV)

For this reason a man will leave his father and mother and be united to his wife, and they will become one flesh. (Genesis 2:24, NIV)

But I tell you that anyone who divorces his wife, except for marital unfaithfulness, causes her to become an adulteress, and anyone who marries the divorced woman commits adultery.

(Matthew 5:32, NIV)

But since there is so much immorality, each man should have his own wife, and each woman her own husband.

(1 Corinthians 7:2, NIV)

Marriage should be honored by all, and the marriage bed kept pure, for God will judge the adulterer and all the sexually immoral.

(Hebrews 13:4, NIV)

Husbands, in the same way be considerate as you live with your wives, and treat them with respect as the weaker partner and as heirs with you of the gracious gift of life, so that nothing will hinder your prayers. (1 Peter 3:7, NIV)

Scriptures for Love

No one has ever seen God; but if we love one another, God lives in us and his love is made complete in us. (1 John 4:12, NIV)

And this is my prayer: that your love may abound more and more in knowledge and depth of insight. (Philippians 1:9, NIV)

So that Christ may dwell in your hearts through faith. And I pray that you, being rooted and established in love, May have power, together with all the saints, to grasp how wide and long and high and deep is the love of Christ, And to know this love that surpasses knowledge--that you may be filled to the measure of all the fullness of God.(Ephesians 3:17-19, NIV)

But the fruit of the Spirit is love, joy, peace, patience, kindness, goodness, faithfulness.(Galatians 5:22, NIV)

The entire law is summed up in a single command: "Love your neighbor as yourself." (Galatians 5:14, NIV)

And now these three remain: faith, hope and love. But the greatest of these is love. (1 Corinthians 13:13, NIV)

Love is patient, love is kind. It does not envy, it does not boast, it is not proud. It is not rude, it is not self-seeking, it is not easily angered, it keeps no record of wrongs. Love does not delight in evil but rejoices with the truth. It always protects, always trusts, always hopes, always perseveres. Love never fails. But where there are prophecies, they will cease; where there are tongues, they will be stilled; where there is knowledge, it will pass away.

(1 Corinthians 13:4-8, NIV)

My command is this: Love each other as I have loved you.
(John 15:12, NIV)

Scriptures for Love

"As the Father has loved me, so have I loved you. Now remain in my love." (John 15:9, NIV)

Jesus replied, "If anyone loves me, he will obey my teaching. My Father will love him, and we will come to him and make our home with him." (John 14:23, NIV)

He answered: "'Love the Lord your God with all your heart and with all your soul and with all your strength and with all your mind'; and, 'Love your neighbor as yourself.'"
(Luke 10:27, NIV)

But I tell you: Love your enemies and pray for those who persecute you. (Matthew 5:44, NIV). How much more for your spouse.

The LORD appeared to us in the past, saying: "I have loved you with an everlasting love; I have drawn you with loving-kindness." (Jeremiah 31:3, NIV)

Scriptures for Trust

Those who know your name will trust in you, for you, LORD, have never forsaken those who seek you. (Psalms 9:10, NIV)

"I "I am the LORD, the God of all mankind. Is anything too hard for me? (Jeremiah 32:27, NIV)

"Ah, Sovereign LORD, you have made the heavens and the earth by your great power and outstretched arm. Nothing is too hard for you." (Jeremiah 32:17, NIV)

For I know the plans I have for you," declares the LORD, "plans to prosper you and not to harm you, plans to give you hope and a future. (Jeremiah 29:11, NIV)

"But blessed is the man who trusts in the LORD, whose confidence is in him. He will be like a tree planted by the water that sends out its roots by the stream. It does not fear when heat comes; its leaves are always green. It has no worries in a year of drought and never fails to bear fruit." (Jeremiah 17:7-8, NIV)

Trust in the LORD forever, for the LORD, the LORD, is the Rock eternal. (Isaiah 26:4, NIV)

Surely God is my salvation; I will trust and not be afraid. The LORD, the LORD, is my strength and my song; he has become my salvation. (Isaiah 12:2, NIV)

Whoever gives heed to instruction prospers, and blessed is he who trusts in the LORD. (Proverbs 16:20, NIV)

Those who trust in the LORD are like Mount Zion, which cannot be shaken but endures forever. (Psalms 125:1, NIV)

Scriptures for Trust

He who dwells in the shelter of the Most High will rest in the shadow of the Almighty. I will say of the LORD, "He is my refuge and my fortress, my God, in whom I trust."
(Psalms 91:1-2, NIV)

Chapter

10

Flourishing Marriages Resources

Visit www.flourishingmarriages.com/products to
purchase additional products.

PRODUCT LIST

Couple's Prayer Declaration

Couple's Declaration Bookmark

Triple O – Real Talk
(Manual, Men's Guide, Women's Guide & DVD Set)

Contact Flourishing Marriages

For information about special discounts for bulk purchases or to book an event, please contact Flourishing Marriages, LLC at 816-287-0567 or flourishingmarriages@yahoo.com.

You can also follow Drs. James and Angel Byrd, affectionately known as "The Love Byrds" via web:

www.flourishingmarriages.com

Twitter:
@TheLoveByrds

Facebook:
https://www.facebook.com/flourishing.marriages
https://www.facebook.com/millionmarriagepicnic

About The Authors

Dr. James & Dr. Angel Byrd
THE LOVE BYRDS

THELOVEBYRDS

■■■■■■■■■■■■■■■■■■■■■■■■■■■■■■■■■■■■■■■

MARRIAGE COUNSELING DUO | AUTHORS | SPEAKERS | RADIO PERSONALITIES

DRS. JAMES & ANGEL BYRD, affectionately known as, **"The Love Byrds"**, are the devoted parents of three beautiful children; Teairra Byrd, Joy Byrd, and James Byrd II. The two have been married for more than 23 years and currently reside in Overland Park, KS. The Love Byrds hold doctorate degrees from **Faith Bible College** of Independence, MO, a local extension of **Oral Roberts University**. With over 17 years of experience, the two are quickly becoming one of the nations most rare and sought after faith-based **marriage and family counseling duos**. Together, they are the founders of the rapidly growing organization and private practice, **Flourishing Marriages LLC**.

A **love for dancing** brought these two together in the night clubs of Kansas City. After becoming friends and dance partners, they chose the same road many travel while living in darkness and without Christ. In 1990, after being invited to a Sunday morning church service, James & Angel answered the call of their Lord and Savior Jesus Christ and were married shortly after.

Though The Love Byrds left night clubs behind them after giving their lives to Christ, their love for dancing remains a major theme of **Flourishing Marriages events, retreats, and marriage**

seminars. Married couples across the nation have grown to expect **five-star venues, fine cuisine, elegant décor & lighting, amorous music**, and **dancing the night away** at every Flourishing Marriages event. In addition to hosting their own events, Drs. James & Angel Byrd were the hosts of popular 890AM talk-radio show, *All the Way Live with the Love Byrds*. Once a week, their chemistry ignited on air to offer invaluable advice and Q & A on marriage and the family for singles, divorced, and married couples alike. The Love Byrds are also the founders of the annual **National Million Marriage Picnic**.

This event unites couples across the nation for one romantic picnic in the park, in all cities across the country, all at the same time. The National Million Marriage Picnic is the first event of it's kind, meant to be a bold display of marriage God's way.

For the past 17 years the Byrd home has not only been a place of refuge and ministry for youth; but together God has used the two **to reunite separated and divorced couples, lead couples living together in sin to the altar of marriage**, and to **promote unity amongst couples struggling to live harmoniously**. Truly possessing a **passion for seeing families thrive**, the two mentored couples without charge for many years. It was not until they sought God for revelation of their purpose in life that the two realized they were called to marriages and pursued formal education.

www.ingramcontent.com/pod-product-compliance
Lightning Source LLC
Chambersburg PA
CBHW070025110426
42741CB00034B/2591